Walk Together Children

Student

Robin Harris Kimbrough

Abingdon Press/Nashville

Walk Together, Children: Taking a Stand for God

Student Book

Marilyn E. Thornton, Lead Editor

Copyright 2007 by Abingdon Press

All rights reserved.

This book is printed on acid-free, elemental-chlorine-free paper.

Library of Congress Cataloging-in-Publication Data
ISBN 978-0-687-49087-5

07 08 09 10 11 12 13 14 15 16 — 10 9 8 7 6 5 4 3 2 1

MANUFACTURED IN THE UNITED STATES OF AMERICA

CONTENTS

INTRODUCTION

This Bible study, *Walk Together, Children: Taking a Stand for God,* had its inception in two trains of thought. One came directly from a study conducted by the Southeastern Jurisdiction Conference of Ethnic Local Church Concerns of the United Methodist Church. The study indicated that Christians needed a medium by which to discuss:

1. The history of racism in the Church Universal

2. How the legacy of the past is affecting the present

3. Thinking theologically about justice and reconciliation

4. Learning behaviors that create change

5. How to be peacemakers in a multicultural world.

It was felt that much has been unresolved and that a Church that remains divided by racism and injustice is hampered in carrying out the work of the Great Commission, to spread the good news of Jesus Christ and make disciples for him.

The other train of thought came by way of a publication from the Veterans of Hope Project: A Center for the Study of Religion and Democratic Renewal, based at Iliff School of Theology in Denver, Colorado. This project focused on the lives of persons who have dedicated themselves in word and deed to social transformation. Through interviews, historian Vincent Harding offers these strategists, warriors, organizers, and movers of the mid-twentieth–century Freedom Movement as encouragement for twenty-first–century post-moderns to continue the realization of the beloved community, God's reign right now! The five from the project who are featured in this study are James Lawson, Ruby Sales, Bernice Johnson Reagon, Andrew Young, and Dolores Huerta.

These two elements have been skillfully woven together in lessons that keep interest during the designated Bible Study time and offer items for continuing engagement of mind, body, and spirit for future weeks and months. There has been much discussion about the nature of evangelism and how to get Christians to share the Gospel of Jesus Christ in ways that are meaningful to themselves and to those who have yet to knowingly experience God's saving grace in their lives. *Walk Together, Children: Taking a Stand for God* is created and designed to provide a stimulus by which participants can discuss history and twenty-first–century issues, utilizing the faith-filled, sanctified lives of heroes for justice. This will help others to make the connection that God's salvation is for all people everywhere, for now and through eternity.

Marilyn E. Thornton
Lead Editor of African American Resources
Contributing Editor for *Walk Together, Children*

STEPPING OVER BARRIERS

Joshua 3:14-17; 4:4-7, 11

Key Verse

When the people set out from their tents to cross over the Jordan, the priests bearing the ark of the covenant were in front of the people. (Joshua 3:14)

Quotable Quote

I know one thing we did right, was the day we started to fight; keep your eyes on the prize, hold on! (Civil rights anthem)

BIBLE LESSON

When the people set out from their tents to cross over the Jordan, the priests bearing the ark of the covenant were in front of the people. Now the Jordan overflows all its banks throughout the time of harvest. So when those who bore the ark had come to the Jordan, and the feet of the priests bearing the ark were dipped in the edge of the water, the waters flowing from above stood still, rising up in a single heap far off at Adam, the city that is beside Zarethan, while those flowing towards the sea of the Arabah, the Dead Sea, were wholly cut off. Then the people crossed over opposite Jericho. While all Israel were crossing over on dry ground, the priests who bore the ark of the covenant of the LORD stood on dry ground in the middle of the Jordan, until the entire nation finished crossing over the Jordan.

Then Joshua summoned the twelve men from the Israelites, whom he had appointed, one from each tribe. Joshua said to them, 'Pass on before the ark of the LORD your God into the middle of the Jordan, and each of you take up a stone on his shoulder, one for each of the tribes of the Israelites, so that this may be a sign among you. When your children ask in time to come, "What do those stones mean to you?" then you shall tell them that the waters of the Jordan were cut off in front of the ark of the covenant of the LORD. When it crossed over the Jordan, the waters of the Jordan were cut off. So these stones shall be to the Israelites a memorial for ever.' As soon as all the people finished crossing over, the ark of the LORD, and the priests, crossed over in front of the people.

AIN'T GONNA LET NOBODY TURN ME 'ROUND

The words to the old spiritual were:

Don't you let nobody turn you 'round,
turn you 'round, turn you 'round.
Don't you let nobody turn you 'round.
Keep on a-walkin', keep on a-talkin', marchin' on to Canaan land.

They expressed a determination to keep on keeping on to see what the end would be. Despite the difficulties of being Christian in an oppressive, racist situation, the slave ancestors would not let any barrier stand in their way to living in God's realm. The leaders of the Civil Rights Movement had a similar claim. No matter the barriers and no matter the temptations to turn back or to turn to violence, they were determined to lead the people to a place promised not only by the Constitution of the United States but by a Savior who preached the good news of a kingdom of love, deliverance, and justice for all.

THE BETTER WAY (Joshua 3:14)

Barriers often block our way to God's promises in life. After many years of following Moses, the people of Israel must now follow Joshua. They were preparing to cross over the Jordan River into the Promised Land. In leading the people, Joshua needed to use a strategy that would enable the people to safely cross over the barrier of the Jordan River. The people were depending on Joshua, whose strategy came from God. The plan for crossing was not the only way to do it, but it was the better way because it was God's way.

> *The LORD said to Joshua, "This day I will begin to exalt you in the sight of all Israel, so that they may know that I will be with you as I was with Moses."* (Joshua 3:7)

The Rev. Dr. James Morrison Lawson Jr. is a Civil Rights leader and pioneer in the fight against racism and other injustices. The framework out of which Dr. Lawson operated was one based upon the teachings of Jesus Christ. Like Joshua, Dr. Lawson and other Civil Rights pioneers could talk directly to God. Additionally, they relied on Scripture and experience to develop strategies around racism and other issues. Joshua had to plan a strategy to lead thousands of people across the Jordan. Dr. Lawson and other

Civil Rights leaders led thousands of people across racism and the institution of segregation. Although these leaders had different sets of challenges, they both are examples of how the ability to lead and strategize to find the better way is based in God's plan.

Lawson's beliefs were partially inspired by life experience. As a child, while on an errand for his mother, another boy called him that hated word (n-----). In response to this racial insult, he slapped the boy. When Lawson told his mother, she asked him, "What did that accomplish?" This response showed him that there was a better way to deal with racism than violence.

Despite having a father who, even as an A.M.E. pastor, carried a gun lest someone should disrespect him as a black man, Lawson came to believe that the better way was love. In 1947, as a freshman in college, he became a part of FOR (Fellowship of Reconciliation), an organization dedicated to the application of love as a means for change. The motto of FOR was "Love is a way of life" that must be applied in all areas. He spent fourteen months in prison because for him, following love as a way of life meant not participating in war (Korean). After finishing college, he went to India as a campus minister for the Methodist Church, where he absorbed the teachings of Mahatma Ghandi. Upon returning to the states, he enrolled in divinity school and began teaching the principles of passive resistance and nonviolence to students in Nashville. He was merely seeking "to follow Jesus," using the better way of love.

Blessed are the peacemakers, for they will be called children of God. (Matthew 5:9)

SAME STORY, DIFFERENT SCRIPT

God assured Joshua of safe passage in crossing the Jordan. Safe passage through a body of water was an event that would be recognized by the people of Israel. Just as Moses had led their ancestors through the Red Sea, Joshua was leading them through the Jordan River. It was the same story but a different script. Instead of the Red Sea, it was the Jordan River separating them from God's promise of deliverance. Nevertheless, deliverance was coming from the same God, who had been and would be faithful over many generations.

Walk about Zion, go all around it,
count its towers,
consider well its ramparts;
go through its citadels,
that you may tell the next generation
that this is God,
our God forever and ever.
He will be our guide forever. (Psalm 48:12-14)

Slavery and segregation, too, were the same story, but different scripts. Both systems were designed to dehumanize black people and maintain white supremacy through laws and religious teachings. The trans-Atlantic slave trade, which stretched from Africa to Europe to the Americas, was based on an ideology that black people were destined to be slaves. There were many Whites that did not think that Blacks even had souls, and so the evangelistic effort among the slaves was often non-existent. Slaves were converted to Christianity in many different denominations, however, with the camp meetings in the Baptist and Methodist traditions being more attractive and hospitable among the slaves. Nevertheless, all forms of Christianity struggled with the same issue. Slaves were converted by the Gospel but not physically freed by it. Most Whites did not recognize Africans as fully human, therefore as deserving of freedom. Writings like the Willie Lynch papers provided techniques of oppression that helped masters maintain physical and psychological control. Laws were created to prevent the manumission of slaves due to conversion.

As a result, whenever they could, enslaved and freed Blacks formed their own churches. In 1776, First Baptist Church in Williamsburg, Virginia, became the first church organized by Blacks for Blacks. It consisted of slave and free Africans. In Philadelphia, Richard Allen and others, in response to racist treatment (separation into galleries and refusal of ordination privileges to Blacks), began a process that would establish the African Methodist Episcopal Church in 1816. There were other moves in Delaware with Peter Spencer and in New York with James Varick. From the formation of the Colored (Christian) Methodist Episcopal Church in 1870 to the formation of the National Baptists in 1895, separation due to racism and a lack of love for God's humanity has been the order of the day. Even in the twenty-first century, worship services remain the most segregated component in our society. Despite the appearance of interdenominational churches and efforts to bring about racial healing, very few churches have a well-balanced blend of ethnic groups, and most resist the idea.

After this I looked, and there was a great multitude that no one could count, from every nation, from all tribes and peoples and languages, standing before the throne and before the Lamb, robed in white, with palm branches in their hands. (Revelation 7:9)

When slavery ended with the passage of the Thirteenth and Fourteenth Amendments, segregation emerged. It was a different script, but the same story. Jim Crow laws continued the legality of racism, giving Whites privileged status and maintaining that black people were not fully human by denying them civil liberties and equal accommodations. Religion continued to play its role in promoting systemic and structural racism. Movies like "Birth of a Nation" showed the Ku Klux Klan as being a Christian organization that was doing the work of God.

THE PROCESS AND STRATEGY (Joshua 3:15-17; 4:11)

Fighting against barriers, whether geography or social systems, requires a strategy and leaders who will hear from God on carrying out that strategy. God's presence with Joshua enabled the people to have faith in his leadership and his plan. God wanted the Hebrew people to cross the Jordan River in an orderly manner. The priests, carrying the Ark of the Covenant, walked out first into the water. They were stepping out into God's grace. Once the soles of the feet of the priests touched the water, the Jordan River backed up, leaving a dry riverbed over which the people could cross. The priests remained in the middle of the Jordan until the entire nation crossed. All of the people made it into the Promised Land, not merely a talented tenth.

Dr. Lawson's search for the better way was only the threshold. Dr. Lawson had to convince others to step over into a new way of thinking in order to practice civil disobedience and nonviolence. Change would not come in an instant. He and other leaders were attempting to correct centuries of faulty theological thought, showing that denial of civil liberties to a certain race was not Christ-like. Those who demonstrated needed transformation as well, coming into a realization that black people were truly children of God who could show love to self and to others through orderly, nonviolent demonstrations. Demonstrators in the Nashville campaign included students from American Baptist College (such as John Lewis and Bernard Lafayette) and Fisk University (such as Diane Nash and Marion Barry). The process involved training people to do sit-ins and developing participants who believed in the strategy. While the first sit-ins actually occurred in

Greensboro, North Carolina, on February 1, 1960, Nashville was the first southern city to desegregate its public facilities because of the disciplined, persistent strategy led by James Lawson.

6, 12, 21 (Joshua 4:4-7)

Upon crossing the Jordan, God had directed Joshua to collect twelve stones representing the twelve tribes of Israel and place them near the camp as a reminder to future generations of how God had crossed them over. Twenty-first–century Christians must also remember the struggles of the past. For us, the twelve stones represent the body of Christ and God's desire for us to live in racial unity. Each stone is different—every tribe has its particularities—but each is formed in God's image with a right to God's deliverance and promise. All of the Hebrew tribes were successful in crossing the Jordan River into the Promised Land. Such an outcome required a particular kind of leadership.

Those in leadership must be submissive to the will of God. In looking for persons to lead demonstrations in Nashville, Lawson sought serious leaders who, like Joshua, were willing to release their fear to God and to meditate on the law day and night. Although many persons were asked to join the movement, only a certain segment would qualify to be leaders in the movement. Lawson wanted people who could see the spiritual and moral base of nonviolence, experiencing it as a way of life. Diane Nash, for example, was a devout Catholic who went to Mass every morning, praying for strength as she led the students in Nashville. Too often leaders lose their credibility because they do not let the Spirit lead them; they try to lead the Spirit. To be a good leader, one must follow the Spirit of God for the long term.

Racial injustice continues in our churches and in society. When charged with the same first-time offense, a young black man is eight times more likely to be imprisoned than a white person. The situation of the Jena 6 in Louisiana is a good example of how African Americans continue to be subject to uneven treatment in the courts. In this case, the young white men who hung the nooses in the schoolyard were not even charged with a hate crime. When they perpetrated violence on the black children, there was no punishment; yet six young black men were charged as adults and imprisoned when they turned to violence in an attempt for justice. While a popular syndicated radio talk show host led the charge that took thousands to Jena, in the midst of the controversy James Lawson was teaching the principles of nonviolence to students who chose to participate. He was showing them how to cross the barriers of anger within themselves by not turning to violence, even under stress. Lawson showed them that the strategies, principles, and processes of former years were still relevant to the situation and useful for the generation of the twenty-first century. God's grace is always appropriate. God's Spirit will provide the power to move all the people into the promises of God.

Principles of Nonviolence
1. Resists evil and oppression.
2. Seeks to win the friendship and understanding of the opponent—not to humiliate or defeat.
3. Attacks the forces of evil, not the person.
4. Is based on love; includes loving one's opponent.
5. The person who practices nonviolence believes in the future, that some day justice will triumph.

FOR DISCUSSION
1. How does the situation of the Hebrew children compare with that of African Americans in the mid-twentieth century?

2. What have been some of the barriers in your life?

3. What is the best way to overcome obstacles and barriers?

4. Did you participate or do you know someone who participated in passive resistance demonstrations?

5. How does faith in Jesus Christ affect one's ability to hope for justice?

6. What are some current situations in your community that need the radical love of Jesus Christ?

WALKING IN THE LIGHT

Proverbs 6:20-23
Key Verse
When you walk, they will lead you.
(Proverbs 6:22a)

Quotable Quote
When you let your own light shine, others will do the same (alt.).
(Made famous by Nelson Mandela)

BIBLE LESSON

My child, keep your father's commandment,
and do not forsake your mother's teaching.

Bind them upon your heart always;
tie them around your neck.

When you walk, they will lead you;
when you lie down, they will watch over you;
and when you awake, they will talk with you.

For the commandment is a lamp and the teaching a light,
and the reproofs of discipline are the way of life.

THIS LITTLE LIGHT OF MINE

When persons lifted this song in the 1960s, it was more than just a cute ditty; it was a song that empowered people to believe that God's light was truly shining on them and in them to move forward in faith and in life. The elders shielded their children as much and as long as possible from the terrors of a racist society; however, the Church itself was often no help. From the split of denominations over slavery (1843–44), to the establishment of separate areas for worship, to the creation of the Central Jurisdiction (Methodist Episcopal) in 1939, black Christians suffered the pain of exclusion and hatred in a place that should have exuded the light of God's love and acceptance for all. By singing "This Little Light of Mine" through the generations, the elders were able to pass on to their children that they were indeed somebody, no matter the message they received from the world or even the Church.

IT STARTS AT HOME

The book of Proverbs is a book of Wisdom. Many of the proverbs are attributed to Solomon. This book is a guide to daily living, how to function in relationships, how to relate to one's family, and the importance of a strong work ethic. There are wise sayings, like African proverbs, that make you think about and laugh at human behavior. Proverbs 6:20-23 remind us of the huge responsibility of being a parent or a parental figure, admonishing children to keep both mother's and father's rules in their hearts as they mature into adulthood. They show the power of parental direction. Although parents often think their words go in one ear and out the other, the children are really listening. They may not practice these teachings immediately, but as they mature and awaken to the realities of life, they remember. The light turns on. The unappreciated teachings and disciplines of home come into practice as children become adults and parents. Despite the media and the peer group, twenty-first–century parents still have the most influence in the ethical and spiritual formation of their children, for better or for worse!

What the child says, he has learned at home. (African proverb)

TEACH THE CHILDREN

Ruby Sales is a social activist and historian. She understands how her elders influenced her to become involved during the Civil Rights Movement as a sixteen-year-old college student. The lessons she learned as a child and teenager gave her wisdom and strength to make conscious choices to sacrifice for her community. She remembers her mother singing while cleaning the house and recalls her father's deep prayers. Growing up in the Black Church (Baptist), the songs connected her to past generations, moving her from one historical period to the present. Through religion, her family sheltered her from the ills of society; they kept her safe and taught her about God and the importance of community.

Sales' family and community relationships illustrate the African proverb, "It takes a village to raise a child." The elders in her life had always affirmed, protected, and built up her self-esteem. So when she encountered the hatred of white people, she could not believe it. She had not experienced this kind of hatred. However, the lessons she learned had prepared her for the struggle and enabled her to withstand even the threat of death. She says, "One of the very disturbing things for me as a historian is the revisionist spirit that went into the civil rights movement and the kinds of ways in which young people have been robbed of a positive image of that experience. It's important that white kids, as well as black kids, as well as brown kids, get a different image. And you have to be able to pass on that sense to children so that they can also struggle. . . But it's important that we pass along to our young the possibility of what can change through struggle."* As many passages in the Bible indicate, elders need to teach the children historical lessons, teach them about God's grace, teach them to love themselves, and make them feel loved, so that whatever the circumstances they encounter in their lives, they will be prepared for struggle.

But take care and watch yourselves closely, so as neither to forget the things that your eyes have seen nor to let them slip from your mind all the days of your life; make them known to your children and your children's children. (Deuteronomy 4:9)

A friend loves at all times, and kinsfolk are born to share adversity. (Proverbs 17:17)

* Quotes are from the Veterans of Hope Project.

CHILDREN ARE LIKE SPONGES

Like sponges, children soak up everything adults do and say. Most adults have experienced moments of catching themselves as they sound like their own parents and teachers did years ago; now, what those elders were saying finally makes sense. These moments prove that adults have a great influence on children. For this reason, what adults do and say around children is very important.

Children are not born racist; they are taught this behavior. They are taught prejudicial attitudes. Children of any color or background repeat comments and emulate behavior they have heard and seen at home and in their communities. Children act out the negative racial attitudes modeled by elders, whether against black people, white people, Koreans, Mexicans, those from the Middle East, or wherever. This phenomenon is why children of alcoholics are most likely to become alcoholics; children of domestic abusers will likely abuse as adults; children of overweight parents are likely to be overweight. Our children are listening and hanging on every word we say; therefore, we must make our words powerful and positive. We must teach our children about God, faith, and the love of Christ through our songs, words, and actions.

Sales believes that her father's response to the war had a great influence on her. "My father did not believe in war. He thought that it was something that big men made small men do and through that ultimately we all suffered from war. My father was a very peace-loving kind of person, a very gentle person. All of that had a great influence on me as a person as I reflect back on my life." As Ruby matured, she gravitated towards passive resistance and nonviolence. Too many children have witnessed violence in the home and carry these experiences in their hearts and on their necks. Adults should serve as positive influences on children, helping their hearts to be full of a love that will combat hatred, enabling them to make a difference in the community.

CHILDREN CAN LEAD

The Church has not been in the forefront of promoting the all-inclusive love of Jesus Christ. Churches generally remain bastions of segregation, either by choice or custom. Even as most churches no longer ban other races from their communities, often no efforts are made to be truly hospitable to those of different racial and cultural backgrounds. People who are different from the majority membership are tolerated only if they assimilate culturally or decline participation in the power structure.

Children can show the way to a different way of being. Consider Ruby Sales' experience. At age seventeen, she postponed her college career to participate in nonviolence demonstrations, often being jailed. In 1965, Sales, along with Jonathan Daniels and others, was arrested in Alabama. Jonathan was white, a student at an Episcopalian seminary in Massachusetts. Upon release, they went into a shop to buy sodas, Ruby leading the way. The shopkeeper greeted them with a gun, declaring that he would blow out her brains. Ruby felt a pull on her clothes that threw her to the ground. The gun blast felled Jonathan, killing him. "No one has greater love than this, to lay down one's life for one's friends" (John 15:13). This man of faith gave up his life for this young black woman. His Christian witness was more than words. And though the trauma of this event basically silenced her for seven months, Ruby's Christian love for him and desire that justice be served sustained her through many death threats to testify in front of an all-white jury on his behalf. These young people exhibited the love of Christ and true acceptance, understanding that there is a price for living out the Gospel.

Little children, let us love, not in word or speech, but in truth and action. (1 John 3:18)

A COMMUNITY OF VOICES

From grandparents to preachers and teachers, Ruby Sales gives credit to many voices that enabled her to become a strong leader for social justice. The voices in the community included the songs of the ancestors. There are all kinds of voices speaking to twenty-first–century youth, who often no longer hear the songs that gave Ruby strength from childhood. Misogynist rap lyrics that devalue women cloud the minds of young people. Lyrics promoting violence and glorifying the drug culture cannot strengthen young people for life. Voices that perpetrate negative images of black people cannot move this generation toward justice and equality. The church community needs to lift its voice, speaking life into young people of every background, encouraging them to think and do the right thing.

Beloved, we are God's children now; what we will be has not been revealed. What we do know is this: when he is revealed, we will be like him, for we will see him as he is. And all who have this hope in him purify themselves, just as he is pure. (1 John 3:2-4)

EVERY CHILD OF GOD NEEDS TO KNOW

The Scripture lesson does not specifically detail which teachings children should learn. However, it does say that the teachings are a light, referring to the illuminating Word of God. God's Word is the foundation of everything that every child of God needs to know. Every child of God needs to feel safe. While parents and community provide this condition, there is a spiritual safety that only God through Jesus Christ can provide. Every child of God needs to know about the grace of God through Jesus Christ. Teaching persons about God gives them a standard for making good choices and understanding that there are consequences for making bad choices.

If you know that he is righteous, you may be sure that everyone who does right has been born of him. See what love the Father has given us, that we should be called children of God. (1 John 2:29–3:1)

Every child of God needs to know the importance of learning. It is never too late to learn. During the Civil Rights Movement, many young people took the opportunity to attend college seriously, realizing that all education does not occur behind ivy-bound walls. The teachings of the elders laid the groundwork for further education. In the twenty-first century, primary, secondary, and collegiate education is critical.

For once you were darkness, but now in the Lord you are light. Live as children of light—for the fruit of the light is found in all that is good and right and true. (Ephesians 5:8-9)

Every child of God needs to know that she or he is created in the image of God and equal to others in society. When their lives are undergirded by a basic understanding of their worth in the eyes of God, others cannot limit them and they can function in a world that has yet to value everyone as equally human. By defining themselves and gaining identity in Christ, when oppression arises and faith-challenging evil confronts them, they will be able to let their lights shine and make choices that glorify God and build up the community.

For it is God who is at work in you, enabling you both to will and to work for his good pleasure. Do all things without murmuring or arguing, so that you may be blameless and innocent, children of God without blemish in the midst of a crooked and perverse generation, in which you shine like stars in the world. (Philippians 2:13-15)

FOR DISCUSSION

1. What are some of the sayings and proverbs that have been handed down in your family or circle of friends?

2. What was something that happened in your early life that made you aware that you were disliked because of your color or culture?

3. What are some of the negative attitudes that you have had about different cultures that may have been passed on to the children in your family circle?

4. Tell about a negative experience that you have had with a person of another culture or race.

5. Tell about a positive or reconciling experience that you have had with a person of another culture or race.

6. Name at least three ways (beyond food, clothes, and shelter) that communicate to a child that he or she is loved.

WALK TOGETHER, CHILDREN

Isaiah 40:3-5, 28-31
Key Verse
They shall run and not be weary, they shall walk and not faint.
(Isaiah 40:31b)

Quotable Quote
My feet are tired but my spirit is resting.
(Montgomery Bus Boycott participant)

BIBLE LESSON

A voice cries out: "In the wilderness prepare the way of the LORD, make straight in the desert a highway for our God. Every valley shall be lifted up, and every mountain and hill be made low; the uneven ground shall become level, and the rough places a plain. Then the glory of the LORD shall be revealed, and all people shall see it together, for the mouth of the LORD has spoken."

Have you not known? Have you not heard? The LORD is the everlasting God, the Creator of the ends of the earth. He does not faint or grow weary; his understanding is unsearchable. He gives power to the faint, and strengthens the powerless. Even youths will faint and be weary, and the young will fall exhausted; but those who wait for the Lord shall renew their strength, they shall mount up with wings like eagles, they shall run and not be weary, they shall walk and not faint.

STICK TOGETHER

The only way to make it through a wilderness is by sticking together! "Walk Together, Children" is a song that makes that challenge. It was sung all through the Movement. During the Montgomery Bus Boycott the people carpooled and walked in groups through the wilderness of a segregated transportation system. They would sing as they walked. One lady said that her feet were tired but her spirit was resting! Twenty-first–century postmoderns have been brought up on instant gratification and been taught an aggressive individualism that leaves community goals in the dust. Even worship and praise has become individualistic, with the singing of a favored few being preferred to congregational singing. The people of God must learn to walk and sing together in a community of faith, and God will send the Holy Spirit to renew strength for the struggles and opportunities ahead.

THE WILDERNESS EXPERIENCE (Isaiah 40:1-5)

This favorite passage of Scripture has words of comfort to the people of Judah who are in exile in Babylon. The prophet Isaiah promises the people that their punishment will have an end, assuring them of God's presence in the barren places they will find upon return to the Promised Land. While the road from Babylon back to Judah is through the desert, wilderness is also a metaphor describing the spiritual and physical condition of the people of God. God's words to Isaiah describe the wilderness—there's no highway, just desert; there are low places and places too high to climb; and the ground is uneven and rough. Wilderness is a place lacking in human communication and devoid of hope. God assures the people that the way of the Lord is under construction. It is a way back to human connection and relationship with God. Obstacles to community will be removed by the power of God's spirit, and all people will have the opportunity to experience the glory of God. God has determined and dictated the kingdom of God for all people.

THE "I" AND THE "WE"

God's words to Isaiah were for a community, not one individual. Throughout biblical history, God deals with collective bodies of people, in particular the Hebrews. God delivers the Hebrews as a nation, time and time again. The verse "Then the glory of the Lord shall be revealed, and all people shall see it together, for the mouth of the Lord has spoken" indicates God's intentions are for community. In a democratic society, even as each individual has one vote, the rights and laws are for "we, the people." For the Civil Rights Movement, just as each individual brought a voice to the cause, the desired outcome was to create a beloved community for all the people. The Movement was a congregational song, and any child of God could join in. In the midst of the singing, the "I" songs become "we" songs, "I Shall Not Be Moved" became "We Shall Not Be Moved," and the glory of the Lord was revealed in collective response to God's grace.

But be filled with the Spirit, as you sing psalms and hymns and spiritual songs among yourselves, singing and making melody to the Lord in your hearts, giving thanks to God the Father at all times and for everything in the name of our Lord Jesus Christ. (Ephesians 5:18b-20)

THE SINGING WARRIOR

A particular voice during the Civil Rights Movement was that of Bernice Johnson Reagon. Known as "The Singing Warrior," she used her voice as a weapon against racial injustice. Singing defined who she was theologically and politically, a song leader who lifted the songs of faith to redefine a position in life. As a child, she was not allowed to sing out loud in church until she had given a confession of faith, and as a young person who became active in the Movement, she flipped the words of the songs of the ancestors to give them a new meaning. She was a student at Albany State College in Georgia when the demonstrations began. At a meeting, she started a traditional spiritual, "Over my head/I see trouble in the air," but she changed "trouble" to "freedom." This moment of epiphany showed Bernice that her life, struggles, and the movement could speak through the songs. She and other SNCC workers began a new tradition of singing freedom songs that revived the people, giving them the strength to continue to move forward.

He put a new song in my mouth,
a song of praise to our God.
Many will see and fear,
and put their trust in the LORD. (Psalm 40:3)

HAVE YOU NOT KNOWN? (Isaiah 40:28-31)

All of us have been in a wilderness. There are wildernesses of drug abuse and domestic violence. There are wildernesses of mental depression and physical illness. There are wildernesses of poverty and war. The Judahites wanted to get out of the wilderness of exile, of being displaced, and of being a minority. In the same way, African Americans in the 1950s and 60s wanted an end to the wilderness of racial oppression and inequality. In the Methodist Episcopal Church this wilderness was reflected by the separation of Negro churches into the Central Jurisdiction (1939–1968). It was hard for people in majority black denominations to understand why African Americans remained. However, as Bishop Leontine Kelly expressed, they believed that the Church truly could not be Christian without black people and white people and all the people created in God's own image operating as an entity. They chose to wait upon the Lord. Those who were willing to persevere with patience in this wilderness experience would witness God's deliverance.

During the Movement, some of the waiting took place in jail. Jail is a wilderness in any society. For black people it was particularly barren. Jail was a place from which black men disappeared, sometimes taken away by lynch mobs and hung without a trial. In the American South, there were prison farms, wherein black men were deprived of their freedom, for sometimes minor offenses or trumped up charges, to pick cotton for the state. Parchman Farm in Mississippi was the most famous of these.

About midnight Paul and Silas were praying and singing hymns to God, and the prisoners were listening to them. Suddenly there was an earthquake, so violent that the foundations of the prison were shaken.... (Acts 16:25-26a)

Bernice Johnson Reagon spent many days in jail. SNCC workers decided to forego bail, refusing to pay unjust fees, and often deferred their college education. They were waiting on the Lord. Being arrested helped Bernice to know what organizing the Christian church must have been like for Paul and Silas (Acts 16:16-40). It came to her that Paul and Silas were like SNCC workers as they sang and prayed. She realized how singing was the primary source of communication, allowing people from diverse backgrounds to come together as one. As they waited in jail, the singing would go on for hours at a time. They would talk in between the singing, but when conversation reached a peak in intensity, showing forth the diversity of their backgrounds and the complexity of the situation, they would begin to sing again. Song was a medium by which the children were able to walk together and not get weary.

THE SAFETY ZONE

Singing helped to bring people to a consciousness that they were actually living in wilderness. No matter how safe a tent seems to be, it is only a small protection against the wild animals of the wilderness. African Americans had created a safety zone for their children in the midst of the hostile wilderness of segregation. They could survive and feel relatively safe in a situation designed to kill them. It was risky to leave the safety zone. Unfortunately, those who remained in the safety zone did not realize how unsafe they were. The safety zone included Jim Crow laws, police brutality, humiliation, and sub-standard housing and education. The safety zone included the "pact" the black community had made with the white community, which was often broken in the blink of an eye, erupting into lynch mobs and repression. While thousands of people participated in the Movement, the reality is that they were the minority. The majority of the people remained in the safety zone. Many people wanted to speak out against racial injustices during the Movement, but felt that the costs were too high. Worry and fear are strongholds that keep people in the wilderness of the safety zone.

Upon leaving the safety zone by becoming a leader in the Movement, Bernice Johnson Reagon discovered God's constant presence, true safety in the arms of Jesus. Churches, ministers, deacons, and church mothers welcomed the demonstrators. The presence of the Church assured her that what she was doing was sacred, and she felt safe. The singing and sense of community connected her to something greater than the comforts of the safety zone. When Bernice stepped out of the safety zone, she entered into another level of spirituality, which showed up in her singing, enabling her to become an instrument for change. It gave her a sense of security knowing that God was present with her as God spoke through her voice in song. God renewed her strength and gave wings to her voice, which in turn strengthened and inspired a movement. When we are willing to let go of worry and fear, God will give us a new song and our strength will be renewed.

WHAT DO YOU DO WHEN YOU COME OUT OF THE WILDERNESS?

Coming out of the wilderness is not an instant process. Those who come out of the wilderness have a responsibility to free others and encourage them to step out of their imagined safety zones. When Jesus stepped out of the wilderness after being tempted by the devil for forty days and nights, he immediately began doing ministry, announcing his mission to the world.

> *Then Jesus, filled with the power of the Spirit, returned to Galilee, and a report about him spread through all the surrounding country. He began to teach in their synagogues and was praised by everyone.* (Luke 4:14-15)

SNCC workers had to go back to school in order to reap the full benefits of the Movement. Bernice Johnson Reagon earned a Ph.D. from Howard University, taught at American University, and became a curator at the Smithsonian Institute. For thirty years, she continued to sing about justice and embody the movement of God as the founder and artistic director of Sweet Honey in the Rock, an *a capella* group. Reagon's decision to leave a full scholarship at Spelman, and risk her life and well being for the Movement, positioned her to see the glory of the Lord and to fulfill God's purpose for her life.

Despite the achievements of the Civil Rights Movement, many young people hear voices that keep them in the wilderness of non-achievement, violent and sexualized behavior, and self-hatred. These voices do not bring redemption or empower them to use their bodies, minds, and spirits in ways that glorify God. The elders of the community bear a special burden to lead children out of the wilderness, giving them high expectations, helping them to fly like eagles, and removing obstacles so that they can see the glory of the Lord. The former successes and triumphs over oppression are means to help someone else. Nor is the battle fully won. This is what we must do when we come out of the wilderness. God delivered us that we might lead others to God's deliverance, teaching them to walk together and sing together, building up the community of faith.

> *Praise the LORD!*
> *Sing to the LORD a new song,*
>   *his praise in the assembly of the faithful.* (Psalm 149:1)

FOR DISCUSSION

1. How does singing in a community of faith affect you?

2. Tell some instances wherein people in your family or community stuck together to accomplish a goal.

3. How did the demonstrators reverse the stigma of going to jail during the Civil Rights Movement?

4. What is meant by a "pact" that existed between the white community and the black community in the days before the Movement?

5. Are there other artists, musicians, poets, or actors who provided spiritual leadership for positive change?

6. How can people of varying backgrounds learn to worship together and work together for justice?

STEP BY STEP

Luke 18:1-8
Key Verse
*And will not God grant justice to his chosen ones
who cry to him day and night? (Luke 18:7)*

Quotable Quote
If there is no struggle, there is no progress. Agitate, agitate, agitate!
(Frederick Douglass)

BIBLE LESSON
*Then Jesus told them a parable about their need to pray always and not to
lose heart. He said, "In a certain city there was a judge who neither feared
God nor had respect for people. In that city there was a widow who kept
coming to him and saying, 'Grant me justice against my opponent.' For a
while he refused; but later he said to himself, 'Though I have no fear of God
and no respect for anyone, yet because this widow keeps bothering me, I will
grant her justice, so that she may not wear me out by continually coming.'"
And the Lord said, "Listen to what the unjust judge says. And will not God
grant justice to his chosen ones who cry to him day and night? Will he delay
long in helping them? I tell you, he will quickly grant justice to them. And
yet, when the Son of Man comes, will he find faith on earth?"*

O FREEDOM

A story* is told concerning the marches in Birmingham, Alabama, which were headquartered at the Sixteenth Street Baptist Church. Rev. Andrew Young was in charge of the strategy, and he split the young marchers (children and teens) into groups, giving them signs and sending the first group down a specific route. They went out singing "O Freedom." The police motorcycles and paddy wagons were waiting for them. They were arrested. Then Young sent out another group; they took a different route, opposite of the first group, and got to the appointed place. Such was the persistence and determination of this prayer-filled movement! Such was the intelligence of its leaders! Such was the connection from generation to generation that young people, following the directions of leaders, went out singing the ancestral song:

> *O freedom, O freedom, O freedom over me.*
> *And before I'll be a slave*
> *I'll be buried in my grave*
> *And go home to my Lord and be free.*

WHO DESERVES JUSTICE? (Luke 18:1-3)

Jesus told many parables, using real-life stories to explain concepts of God's grace and mercy. He wanted his disciples to understand the need to be persistent in prayer and to never stop trying to make things right. This story involves a paradox. There is a widow seeking justice from an unjust judge. The paradox is that judges are not supposed be unjust. How can justice come from a judge who is unjust? The purpose of judicial systems is to resolve conflict, to identify legal wrongs and make them right. Its methodology is to make sure people are treated fairly. The widow in this story is appearing *pro se*; she is representing herself in her case. She is not taken seriously by the community or by the judge. The woman is not protected because she is a widow; she is a member of a marginalized community. During this time, a woman with no man had very little protection. Only a fatherless child was more vulnerable than a widow. From the law to the prophets, righteous living included extending mercy and justice to widows because they were so vulnerable.

*from *Freedom's Children: Young Civil Rights Activists Tell Their Own Stories* by Ellen Levine, NY: Puffin Books, 2000, p. 87.

When you reap your harvest in your field and forget a sheaf in the field, you shall not go back to get it; it shall be left for the alien, the orphan and the widow.... When you beat your olive trees, do not strip what is left; it shall be left for the alien, the orphan and the widow. (Deuteronomy 24:19a, 20)

Learn to do good; seek justice, rescue the oppressed, defend the orphan, plead for the widow. (Isaiah 1:17)

Do not oppress the widow, the orphan, the alien, or the poor. (Zechariah 7:10a)

The woman in Jesus' story was being oppressed by her situation. She was left to plead for herself. But she had a strategy of persistence. She never let up in her demands for justice even within a system that was inherently unjust towards the females of the community.

If a woman conceives and bears a male child, she shall be ceremonially unclean seven days.... Her time of blood purification shall be thirty-three days. If she bears a female child, she shall be unclean two weeks.... Her time of blood purification shall be sixty-six days. (Leviticus 12:2-5)

Her constant presence was a source of irritation to the judge, who viewed her as undeserving of justice because of gender, economic, and social status.

BE PERSISTENT! (Luke 18:4-6)

African Americans also had to deal with a system that was inherently unjust towards them. From laws that refused black Christians freedom during the colonial times, to the Fugitive Slave Act, which returned slaves who freed themselves by running away to the North, to the Dred Scott Decision, which declared that a black man had no rights that a white man had to honor, black people in America were denied justice. After the landmark 1954 Supreme Court decision, black people prayed and pleaded for justice. Even in the twenty-first century the poor, people of color, domestic violence victims (women), immigrants, children who are abused or neglected, and senior citizens—those who have the least ability and resources to constantly go to court—are often denied justice. These groups are often looked upon by the power structure like the unjust judge looked at the widow. Yet she remained persistent.

The widow knew that she was entitled to justice, and this sense of entitlement did not let her give up hope. Despite the fact that the judge had no fear of God or of any one else, he realized that she would never stop trying. She was going to keep on keeping on. She retained her hope. This is one of the principles of nonviolence, that those who use it as a strategy have hope that justice will be done. Like the widow and persons who participated in the Freedom Movement, we must remain persistent, demanding what is right, regardless of the level of marginalization. We must continue to have hope in the promises of God.

FROM INVESTIGATION TO RECONCILIATION
(Luke 18:7-8)

The reason the widow in the parable sought the assistance of a judge was because she and another person could not reach an agreement. They could not reconcile. This is why most people go to court, as witnessed on judicial reality television shows. The cases in these small-claims disputes involve more than monetary damages. Most litigants come to court with hurt, anger, and unforgiveness in their hearts that distort their perception of justice. In front of the judge, they talk more about their emotions than the real issues. Their emotions will not allow them to hear or understand the other person. As a result, they cannot work it out by themselves. Nor do they have a strategy about how to negotiate an agreement.

Andrew Young was one of the principal strategists and negotiators in the Movement. After college, he had begun to realize that there was more to life than becoming part of the "black bourgeoisie." He answered a call to ministry in the United Church of Christ wherein he committed himself to serve God's people and make the life of Christ real to the world. Once he targeted a community for change, he was relentless in applying the steps of investigation, negotiation, demonstration, and reconciliation. King and Young would meet with community leaders and people in the power structure before any direct action. Often they discovered that there were white people who were friendly to the cause. When the demonstrations started, reconciliatory efforts were already in progress. The demonstrations created more opportunities for negotiations. Those on the inside who were more conciliatory from the beginning were able to help with negotiations from the inside, convincing others to do what they had sworn not to do— that is, end segregation. Despite the struggle, communities were able to heal and reconcile because the groundwork had been laid.

Situations of injustice can only be changed by strategic, persistent petition. Injustice continues, but those aligned with God must walk up to it and stand up to it, at the same time kneeling before God in prayer. God is *not* aligned with injustice or violence. God will grant justice to those who cry out to God. The story of the persistent widow does not tell us how long it took, only that eventually the judge relented and gave the woman justice. By constantly bringing her plea, praying before the judge, she was able to make him do something he did not want to do: give her justice. Had she become complacent she would have lost out. Complacency is a friend to injustice. Jesus encouraged the people not to lose heart but to continuously pray for deliverance. God's timing is not our timing, but God is just. Those who seek justice must keep the issues of injustice in front of people who are able to make a difference, and God will provide deliverance.

THE GOSPEL IS REAL

Unjust judges are not merely figments of Jesus' imagination; they are real. However, the realness of injustice can show forth the reality of the Gospel, the in-breaking of God's kingdom. In St. Augustine, Florida, Young and others were marching and demonstrating. The Ku Klux Klan became involved. He was beaten up, yet during all of this he had the demonstrators reciting Psalm 23. About a month later, the Civil Rights Bill passed. Young and other demonstrators went back to the coffee shop where the white people were now bound by law to serve them. The woman who served Young started to pour the coffee. He remembers that her hands were shaking in the presence of so many black people and she kept pouring until the cup overflowed. The coffee was in the saucer and she tried to remove it and give him a clean cup but he protested. He wanted her to leave it there. He said, "Thou preparest a table before me in the presence of my enemies. Thou anointest my head with oil till my coffee cup runneth over. Hallelujah! I mean that was a religious experience to have your cup run over after having walked through the valley of the shadow of death."* For Young, the Civil Rights Movement brought the Gospel to life.

* Quotes are from the Veterans of Hope Project.

THE CHURCH HAS NO WALLS

For Andrew Young, all of his work in life was ministry. He and Dr. King saw their ministry as breaking down "the dividing wall of hostility between black and white," and in every role, whether congressman, ambassador, or mayor, Young sought to break down walls through a prayer-filled process that moved from investigation to reconciliation, step by step. For the Gospel to be real in the world, we must practice the message of Jesus. We cannot just talk; we must do it!

What if we applied Young's strategy to twenty-first–century situations, taking the time and energy to investigate and negotiate, laying the groundwork for reconciliation before demonstrating? Our prison systems may go empty, there would be less war and street violence, and certainly there would be fewer judicial reality shows on TV.

What if we applied the Gospel to daily living, operating in the power of God to speak against injustices, to stand up for others, to make a difference? By ignoring the cries of the sinned-against—the oppressed, the poor, the violated, the stranger, the imprisoned—we participate with injustice. When we share the love of God with everyone and operate in faith to help all of God's people who are in need, we become the church without walls. We participate in the kingdom Jesus announced, and we will be ready when the Son of Man comes!

FOR DISCUSSION

1. Have you ever experienced injustice? How did it make you feel?

2. Who are some groups in society that must deal with constant injustice? Describe their situation.

3. How do you know that you are entitled to justice?

4. Step by step, apply the process of investigation, negotiation, demonstration, and reconciliation to a situation in your life, church, or community.

5. Talk about ways in which you see God's kingdom breaking into the world.

6. What are ways in which you can participate with God in breaking downs walls of separation?

WALKING THE WALK

Mark 10:13-16
Key Verse
"Let the children come to me; do not stop them; for it is to such as these that the kingdom of God belongs." (Mark 1:14b)

Quotable Quote
When Jesus Christ asked little children to come to him...
*He said, 'Let **all** children come.'* (Marian Wright Edelman)

BIBLE STORY

People were bringing little children to him in order that he might touch them; and the disciples spoke sternly to them. But when Jesus saw this, he was indignant and said to them, "Let the little children come to me; do not stop them; for it is to such as these that the kingdom of God belongs. Truly I tell you, whoever does not receive the kingdom of God as a little child will never enter it." And he took them up in his arms, laid his hands on them, and blessed them.

I GOT SHOES

I got shoes, you got shoes; all God's children got shoes! What a statement of faith and hope for enslaved persons who in reality did not have shoes but who went through their daily lives barefooted! The feet of those who enslaved them were protected from the pebbles and harsh elements. Shoes symbolized a sense of belonging and worth. And to sing about a God who has shoes for all of God's children is an acknowledgement that God is equitable. It expressed a hope that when God reigns, there is enough for all. Jesus announced a kingdom of healing, justice, love, and well being for all of God's children. It starts with the simplest of things: accepting that every person is a child of God.

THE STATUS AND ROLE OF CHILDREN (Mark 10:13)

The status of children has changed dramatically over the centuries. Not long ago, even in the western world, children were working in factories for long hours and pennies a day. Children were considered as nothing; they had no social standing. In the Roman society of Jesus' time, a father could choose to allow his newborn to die by exposure. This usually happened if the child was a girl. The father could just set her outside, and the child would succumb to a death caused by starvation and weather. In the twenty-first century, child slavery still exists, but in many places the well-being of children is at least considered. Yet childhood is different in negative ways than from the times of our fore-parents. Television and other types of media are growing our children up too fast. Children need an alternative activity; they need the spiritual formation of the love of Jesus Christ.

At the beginning of Mark 10, Jesus was responding to questions from a crowd, from Pharisees, and from his disciples concerning divorce and the dynamics of marriage.

> *He left that place and went to the region of Judea and beyond the Jordan. And crowds again gathered around him; and, as was his custom, he again taught them.* (Mark 10:1)

During this exchange, people were bringing their children to Jesus. The disciples seemed to feel that the children were nuisances. They rebuked the parents. Often, in church when a baby is crying or a child is acting out, someone gives the parent the look that says, "You need to take that baby out of here." The parent, feeling embarrassed, gets up and takes the baby out of church. The child is not accepted as being a child; he or she is a nuisance and must be excluded. Imagine how the parents felt when those whom they expected to help them gain access to Jesus were telling them to get away? They felt rejected. The disciples demonstrated that the children were not worthy to come to Jesus. In so many ways, the people expected to love children rejected them, confirming the same status to children in the kingdom Jesus represented as in the Roman Empire.

LET THE CHILDREN COME (Mark 10:14)

Jesus became "indignant." He did not like the fact that his disciples were excluding people. Jesus wanted them to know that his kingdom included even children, the least and the lost! He corrected the disciples and said to them: "Let the little children come to me; do not stop them; for it is to such as these that the kingdom of God belongs" (Mark 10:14).

> *But many who are first will be last, and the last will be first.* (Mark 10:31)

> *And the king will answer them, 'Truly I tell you, just as you did it to one of the least of these who are members of my family, you did it to me.'* (Matthew 25:40)

Marian Wright Edelman, the founder of the Children's Defense Fund (an advocacy group for the well-being of children) interprets Jesus as meaning this: "When Jesus Christ asked little children to come to him... He said, 'Let *all* children come.'" Social activist Dolores Huerta had a similar opinion. In a day (1947) when black children and white children could not even go the same schools in much of the country, Huerta was bringing people together as a teen in her California hometown.

Huerta's poor neighborhood consisted of Italians, Latinos, African Americans, Chinese, Japanese, Native Americans, Greeks, and Filipinos. She formed a teen center in a storefront building for her diverse circle of friends, which included two white girls, despite the racial attitudes of the power structure. The cops closed the center down because they didn't want to see the white girls hanging around with Filipino, Mexican, and black kids.

This was the sentiment of the time and for years to come, not only in the world, but in the Church. Even black denominations were divided over being an inclusive society in the midst of the Civil Rights Movement. Led by persons like Gardner C. Taylor and Wyatt Tee Walker, the Progressive

National Baptist Convention was born in 1961, separating itself from Black Baptists who felt that Martin Luther King Jr. was incorrect in his approach to justice for all. Even as students at American Baptist College (a National Baptist institution) in Nashville threw themselves into demonstrating, persons within the old power structure of National Baptists (USA, Inc.) were forbidden to participate for fear of losing their jobs.

ENTERING THE KINGDOM (Mark 10:15)

Jesus proposed a radical inclusiveness. He told his disciples, not only does the kingdom belong to children, one cannot enter the kingdom unless one becomes as a child! After Jesus made these comments, he wrapped the children in his arms and blessed them. Jesus determined that those who are considered as nothing in the world are part of the kingdom of heaven: the poor, the humble, the meek, the peacemakers, those without arrogance and pride, those who, like children, are dependent on others for their well-being, those with nothing to lose. The kingdom of heaven belongs to those who admit their dependence on God and who carry out God's will of perfect love. When Jesus extended the invitation, "Let the children come to me," it was an invitation to all of us who walk in humility knowing that no matter how old we get, we are still children of God.

> *If anybody asks you who I am, tell 'em I'm a child of God!*
> (African American spiritual)

A WOMAN OF FAITH

While black people were seeking political and social liberties, farm workers from various backgrounds were focused on economic justice. The Civil Rights Movement was a time that continued the opening up of God's kingdom of inclusive love that Jesus announced.

> *"The Spirit of the Lord is upon me, because he has anointed me to bring good news to the poor... to proclaim release to the captives and recovery of sight to the blind, to let the oppressed go free, to proclaim the year of the Lord's favor."* (Luke 4:18-19)

Dolores Huerta was a woman of faith who took this proclamation seriously. It started with the children. As a teacher, she became concerned over the poverty of her students, whose parents' forty-cents-an-hour jobs as farm workers could not cover the basic needs of their children. Leaving her teaching position, she began organizing farm workers in their fight against economic injustice. A single mother with seven children, she stepped out on faith. The day after she made this decision, she found a sack of groceries on her steps. She took the groceries as God's confirmation that it could be done, and she could do it.

Organization of the farm workers was influenced by the simultaneously occurring Civil Rights Movement. Huerta believed that the work of the farm workers was the most sacred of work because it put food on the tables of the nation. She worked with Cesar Chavez, a renowned organizer who, like James Lawson and Martin Luther King Jr., followed the teachings of Gandhi, using passive resistance and nonviolence to combat economic and racist oppression. The farm workers were Mexican, Puerto-Rican, Jamaican, and Haitian, as well as being white and black Americans.

HANDLING REJECTION

Power in society is maintained through rejection because most people like having the approval of others. Even within the African American community, persons are sometimes rejected based on skin color and hair length or texture. Rejection can destroy lives, keeping persons from fulfilling God's destiny and purpose for them. Huerta and other activists experienced rejection, but they did not allow the rejection to stop them from fighting for the rights of others.

Often times, the people we expect to love us the most are the ones who reject us. The people who brought the children to Jesus did not expect to be rejected. The disciples did not realize the impact they were having on the community of God when they turned away the children. Jesus spent most of his ministry being rejected. We cannot avoid being rejected, but how should we respond to racism, sexism, classism, ageism, and all the other "isms"? Jesus' response to rejection was love and forgiveness. The farm workers and the civil rights workers prayed, fasted, took Holy Communion, and sang the songs of Zion. By grace they were able to respond to the violence and the rejection in love. Rather than being a road to dejection, rejection became God's redirection and protection.

SÍ SE PUEDE! *(see say pooay day)*

"Sí se puede" means "it can be done; we can do it." The "it" to which Huerta refers is the ability to "build a world of justice and democracy." A world of justice, where every person counts because every person is recognized as a child of God, represents the in-breaking of kingdom of God, which Jesus announced. The kingdom of God is not only a future concept; the kingdom of God is right now. Let us embrace it with a childlike spirit. The kingdom of God is realized when each of God's children steps out in faith and participates in God's salvation, sharing God's grace in love with people who need it. The work of James Lawson, Ruby Sales, Bernice Johnson Reagon, Andrew Young, and Dolores Huerta, and their commitment to nonviolence and love in the face of violence and injustice, required a childlike spirit submitted to the will of God. When they started out they were young, but as they matured their commitment to the beloved community, the kingdom of God, never wavered.

Often as we grow older, we become more concerned about risk. This is why young people were at the forefront of the Civil Rights Movement, the Peace Movement (to end the Vietnam War), and the Labor Movement (young people who took over factories to build the labor movement). It was the children who actually desegregated the schools in most cases. Often times it is those who have nothing to lose who organize to end oppression, fight for justice, and bring together communities. Against oppression that tells them that they are nothing, they embrace their ability to participate in God's salvation. However, young and old must walk together. We must walk the walk of the one we claim to follow, Jesus Christ. Purpose is not determined by race, color, class, creed, or age but by our ability to receive and communicate the reign of God in history and throughout eternity. With the help of God through Jesus Christ, by the power of the Holy Spirit, we can do it, share God's love in word and deed!

Sí se puede! Sí se puede! Thy will be done!

FOR DISCUSSION

1. What do images of barefoot African children mean to you?

2. People often complain that they cannot discipline children through spanking anymore, that they may be accused of child-abuse. Do you think that the issues of children's rights and needs are balanced in the twenty-first century?

3. Why is it important to refer to Jesus' announcement about his ministry (Luke 4:16-21) in continuing the conversation about salvation and the kingdom of God?

4. In what socio/economic/political/justice/educational issues is your church involved? Talk about how personal involvement in a socio/economic/political/justice/educational issue helped you to experience the presence of God.

5. Describe an incident in which you experienced or saw someone else experience rejection from an unexpected source.

6. How do you share the good news of God's reign with persons who are of a different culture, background, generation, or economic status than you?